Marine Expeditionary Units

BY LINDA BOZZO

amicus
high interest

Amicus High Interest is an imprint of Amicus
P.O. Box 1329, Mankato, MN 56002
www.amicuspublishing.us

Library of Congress Cataloging-in-Publication Data
Bozzo, Linda.
 Marine Expeditionary Units / by Linda Bozzo.
     pages cm. – (Serving in the military)
 Includes index.
 Summary: "An introduction to the life of a marine in a Marine
Expeditionary Unit (MEU). Describes some of the missions
assigned to MEUs, how they train, and their role in the U.S.
armed forces"– Provided by publisher.
ISBN 978-1-60753-493-8 (library bound) –
ISBN 978-1-60753-636-9 (ebook)
1. United States. Marine Corps–Juvenile literature. 2. Special
forces (Military science)–United States–Juvenile literature. I.
Title.
 VE23.B6189 2015
 359.9′631–dc23

                                              2013039231

Editor: Wendy Dieker
Series Designer: Kathleen Petelinsek
Book Designer: Steve Christensen
Photo Researcher: Kurtis Kinneman

Photo Credits: Stocktrek Images/Alamy, cover; US Air Force -
digital version c/Science Faction/Corbis 5; Stocktrek Images/
Stocktrek Images/Corbis 6; Stephen Barnes/Military/Alamy 9;
US Marines Photo/Alamy 10-11; US Marines Photo/Alamy 13;
Ed Darack/Science Faction/Corbis 14; US Army Photo/Alamy
17; Stocktrek Images/Stocktrek Images/Corbis 18; US Marines
Photo/Alamy 21; Creator: Capt. Caleb Eames 22-23; Capt.
Will Klumpp 25; Lance Cpl. Timothy Childers 26; US Army
Photo/Alamy 29

Printed in the United States at Corporate Graphics in North
Mankato, Minnesota.

10 9 8 7 6 5 4 3 2 1

Table of Contents

Saving Lives

It is April 2012. A Marine Expeditionary Unit (MEU) is training. They are in Morocco. Crash! An Osprey aircraft hits the ground. The cockpit is crushed. The crew is trapped! Fuel is spilling out. It is very dangerous. But marines rush to the crash. They must rescue the crew.

 What is an Osprey?

An Osprey can fly like a plane or a helicopter.

 It is like a chopper and plane in one. The rotors can point up like a helicopter. Or they can point forward like an airplane.

Soldiers work together. They carry a teammate away from danger.

One marine crawls into the Osprey's cockpit. With no tools, he tears through metal and straps. He frees one pilot. The second pilot's leg is trapped. The marine grabs an axe and cuts through the mess. The pilot is free. Other marines come to pull the pilot out.

More marines tear through a small hole in the back. They find two crew chiefs trapped inside. They work hard to free them. But it is too late. These men die from their injuries.

Even in the face of danger, the marines worked hard to save lives. They later received awards for their bravery.

 What award did the marines get?

Soldiers are awarded for bravery. The medals are pinned to uniforms.

 The marines got the Navy and Marine Corps medal. This is the highest award for bravery outside of war.

Elite Training

An MEU is part of the U.S. Marine Corps. It has a little bit of everything that the whole corps has. It is a **task force** with special missions. Only the best marines are asked to be part of an MEU. This means more training.

MEUs train for any task.

MEU training is sometimes called "crawl, walk, run." For six months, marines work hard. They practice skills. They learn how to use special gear. They don't get much rest. The training goes from hard to harder to hardest. Each step builds on what they just learned.

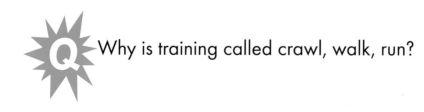

Why is training called crawl, walk, run?

Marines train for missions in water.

Think of a baby that has to crawl before he can walk. Marines have to work on basics before they can move on to harder training.

Many missions take place at night.
Marines learn to fly in the dark.

Marine pilots learn to fly in the dark of night. They know how to fly helicopters and jets. They learn to fly Ospreys. Ground marines drive **AAVs**. These trucks float on water. And they drive on land.

Marines practice shooting rifles and machine guns. They also practice using bombs. They can fire rockets, **grenades**, and **missiles**.

A training mission is just like a real one. MEUs must be sure their teams are ready for anything. They practice **raiding** a building. A fake enemy leader is captured. A fake **hostage** is rescued. Today the teams train. Tomorrow they fight!

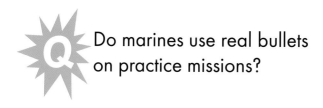
Do marines use real bullets on practice missions?

**These men are ready
to raid a building.**

 No. They usually use fake bullets. This
way, no one gets shot during practice.

These ships carry everything
an MEU needs.

 How many marines are in an MEU?

Overseas

An MEU goes out on three large ships. These marines sail around the world. They are on the ships for about six months. This way, they are close to where they are needed.

The ships carry all the things the MEUs need. They have Ospreys, AAVs, and weapons. It's all there and ready to go.

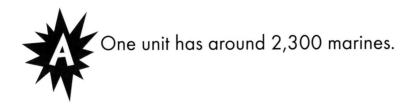
One unit has around 2,300 marines.

When trouble strikes, an MEU will get there first. Other forces will catch up later. An MEU gets an order for a mission. In four hours, they have a plan. Another hour later, their gear is ready. After the sixth hour, the MEU is on the way. It is time for action!

 Do all 2,300 marines go on a mission?

A small group from an MEU goes ahead to check things out.

No. A small task force of a few marines will go to the trouble. Many will stay on the ships to do their jobs.

MEUs are ready for any mission. They rescue hostages. They stop ships to find enemies. They raid buildings.

But MEUs don't just fight. They are the first to help people after a storm or earthquake. They also train soldiers in other countries.

An MEU delivers supplies after a storm.

The Home Front

MEUs return to the home front after six months. When one MEU returns home, the next unit ships out. There is always an MEU ready to go.

For a few months, the marines rest. Equipment is repaired. Any problems with missions are worked out. But then training starts up again. It's back to crawl, walk, run.

A mechanic makes sure a Humvee is ready for the next mission.

A marine gives medical
care to a baby.

The marines are not just about fighting. Their job is also to serve people. On the home front, MEUs help those who need it. They help with food drives. They help build homes. After a hurricane, marines even helped build playgrounds.

Serving Our Country

An MEU can take on any mission. They are always ready. In 2001, enemies from Afghanistan attacked the United States. The marines were ready. An MEU was sent to Afghanistan. They were the first to land. A task force fought the enemy. The MEUs work to keep our country safe.

Marines can make a
quick landing. They can
drop from a chopper.

Glossary

AAV Short for amphibious assault vehicle, a vehicle that can move on land with wheels or tracks and also float in water like a boat.

grenade A small bomb or explosive that can be thrown by hand or shot from a launcher.

hostage Someone who is captured and held by the enemy.

missile A weapon that is thrown or shot and can often reach long distances.

raid A sudden attack.

task force A group of units that perform a specific mission.

Read More

Alvarez, Carlos. *Marine Expeditionary Units.* Minneapolis: Bellwether Media, 2010.

Braulick, Carrie A. *U.S. Marine Expeditionary Units.* Mankato, Minn: Capstone Press, 2006.

Gordon, Nick. *Marine Expeditionary Units.* Minneapolis: Bellwether Media, 2013.

Websites

Inside Today's Military: What is a Marine Expeditionary Unit (MEU)?
www.todaysmilitary.com/inside/view/ what-is-a-marine-expeditionary-unit

Marines: First to Fight: 6 Hours
www.marines.com/operating-forces/first-to-fight/

U.S. Department of Veteran Affairs: VA Kids
www.va.gov/kids/

Every effort has been made to ensure that these websites are appropriate for children. However, because of the nature of the Internet, it is impossible to guarantee that these sites will remain active indefinitely or that their contents will not be altered.

Index

About the Author

Linda Bozzo is the author of more than 45 books for the school and library market. She would like to thank all of the men and women in the military for their outstanding service to our country. Visit her website at www.lindabozzo.com.